Praise for *The Compleat Th_____*

Is Ian Gilbert saner than he ought to be? Is his collection of madness liable to make us all more level-headed? Can he see what was never there in the first place?

The Compleat Thunks Book might well tell the reader more about themselves than they already knew.

I certainly recommend it.

Johnny Ball, TV presenter and science enthusiast

Imagine a world where success isn't getting the answer right, but rather being brave enough to take on the question – allowing a little grapple to develop into a full-on wrestling match before pausing only to laugh out loud at yourself and subsequently find new ground. That's *The Compleat Thunks Book*. It allows, no, actively encourages you to change your mind in the middle of making a point!

It's perfect for getting people off automatic using gentle poking.

Jaz Ampaw-Farr, Director, Why First Ltd, speaker and *The Apprentice* candidate

A fabulously entertaining book.

The Compleat Thunks Book reignites a sense of curiosity and wonder you'd forgotten you had. Whether you read it alone or read it with friends, these Thunks will unleash your inner 'why?' and make you think.

Graham Brown-Martin, author and broadcaster

I love the design, thoughtfulness and impact of these questions. Thunks make you think and often smile – which is a healthy combination for the reader and those on the receiving end of a great question. The variety of questions stimulate the mind and are a great mental workout that should be prescribed daily, or even before every meal.

I wholeheartedly recommend *The Compleat Thunks Book* for school-age philosophers and any adult who is looking for a great mind-stretch.

Andy Gilbert, thinking engineer and
developer of the Go MAD Thinking system

If a major educational illness is dry and arid rote learning, then Thunks are a superb antidote. They encourage true independent thinking.

I have used many of Ian's Thunks with my own sons – usually at their request – and the laughter and debate they have created remains a beautiful memory of their childhood.

Ben Walden, Director, Contender Charlie

This book is about developing wisdom. The reader is required to pause, think and analyse their thoughts before coming to a conclusion – a skill that will be essential for success in the modern world, where we are inundated with false information.

Floyd Woodrow, author of *Elite!* and
The Warrior, the Strategist and You

the
compleat
thunks
book

Ian Gilbert

the compleat thunks book

Independent Thinking Press

First published by

Independent Thinking Press
Crown Buildings, Bancyfelin, Carmarthen,
Wales, SA33 5ND, UK
www.independentthinkingpress.com

Independent Thinking Press is an imprint
of Crown House Publishing Ltd.

A small number of Thunks® in this book have been published in *The Little Book
of Thunks*® (978-184590062-5), *The Book of Thunks*® (978-184590092-2),
Independent Thinking (978-178135055-3), on Twitter (@Thatiangilbert, although
this account is no longer used by Ian Gilbert) and on www.thunks.co.uk.

Thunks® and THUNKS® are registered trademarks of Independent Thinking Ltd.

Independent Thinking Press has no responsibility for the persistence or
accuracy of URLs for external or third-party websites referred to in this
publication, and does not guarantee that any content on such websites is,
or will remain, accurate or appropriate.

British Library Cataloguing-in-Publication Data

A catalogue entry for this book is available from the British Library.

ISBN 978-178135272-4 (print)
ISBN 978-178135285-4 (mobi)
ISBN 978-178135286-1 (ePub)
ISBN 978-178135287-8 (ePDF)

Printed and bound in the UK by Gomer Press, Llandysul, Ceredigion

To all those who have Thunked
before and come to the same
conclusion: my brain hurts.

Thunks – A User's Guide

We live, so they tell us, in a post-fact world. What they omit to tell us is that if we simply accept the fact that there are no facts, we're all doomed.

It used to be that the truth counted a great deal, but now we have new words for the acceptable lies of influential people – 'misremembering' (US news anchor Brian Williams et al.); 'misspeaking' (Hillary Clinton et al.); 'a mistake' (MEP Nigel Farage); 'an aspiration' (MP Chris Grayling); 'an extrapolation' (MP Iain Duncan Smith); 'a rich thesaurus of things that I've said that have ... been misconstrued' (MP Boris Johnson); 'short-circuited' (Hillary Clinton again); 'a series of possibilities' (MP Iain Duncan Smith again); 'mischaracterization of the intelligence' (US government report into the claim that Iraq had weapons of mass destruction); 'not an accurate description of the intelligence' (UK's Chilcot Report on the same); 'an inverted pyramid of piffle' (MP Boris Johnson again); 'alternative facts' (the Trump administration); 'we can disagree with the facts ... Our intention is never to lie to you' (the Trump administration again); 'a euphenism' (Trump himself, using a made-up word to explain the difference between his promises and reality).

Most humans are susceptible to believing what they are told by figures of authority such as parents, teachers, politicians and Rupert Murdoch. Indeed, you can argue that this is how we have survived so long and so well as a species. ('Don't eat that berry.' 'Don't stroke that sabre-toothed tiger.' 'Don't wake your father.') Put an actor with pristine white teeth in a pristine white lab coat and we are more likely to buy their toothpaste/moisturiser/life insurance/range of new lab coats. Put a heavily biased interpretation of the truth in large black letters below a masthead and we buy it, literally and metaphorically.

All of which means that now, more than ever, we need to be asking questions, to be looking deeper, to be challenging those figures of authority, to be becoming obstreperously curious. In short, to be thinking for ourselves.

And, if you agree, then think of Thunks as your thinking training ground.

The way a Thunk works is deceptively simple. It is a question that is specifically designed to elicit any one of the following answers:

1. Yes
2. No
3. Neither

4. Both
5. Something else
6. All of the above
7. None of the above

In other words, it's not about the answers at all and, as in life, there are none at the back of the book. After all, an answer is a door closed, a cul-de-sac to further thinking, the end of the cognitive line and, as such, answers are highly overrated. With a Thunk, the answer is quite simply not as important as the thinking, reasoning, logic or panic employed to arrive at it and to justify (or deviate from) it in any conversation that ensues.

Covering as wide a variation of topics as possible, from love and lies to parking a car and molesting robots, there are Thunks here for all ages, tastes and prejudices. Simply dive in anywhere and start thinking for yourself.

The future of the world depends on it.

The
Thunks

1. Is a broken-down car parked?

2. When you put the sliding roof on a stadium does it become a room?

3. Should prisons be nice places?

4. Are you better at marriage the more you do it?

5. Is there a safe way to die?

6. Can we be sure trees can't think?

7. Is there more future than past?

8. If you accidentally bump into
your dog should you apologise?

9. If it were proven that God exists, would
you still be able to believe in Him (or Her)?

10. Can exercise make you sad?

11. Should we pay criminals not to commit any more crimes?

12. If I take a photo of a photo of you, do I have a photo of you rather than a photo of a photo of you?

13. Is your pet part of your family?

14. Can a baby make art?

15. Is it the space inside
that makes a vase a vase?

16. Is water porous?

17. Do you miss someone more
when they're away from you than
when you're away from them?

18. Is a dead horse a horse?

19. Can you have a premonition about something happening that you then prevent from happening?

20. Is it worse to pretend you're gay than to pretend you're straight?

21. Do you live in your head?

22. If a working class person wins a million pounds are they no longer working class?

23. Do you need to be a parent to be a good teacher?

24. Is it OK to think bad things?

25. Can you know what love
is without being in love?

26. Does human speech
sound like song to a bird?

27. Can a blind person be racist?

28. Is it the same film when it's dubbed?

29. Is it better to love it and
fail it than to ace it and hate it?

30. Has anyone who owns a Ferrari ever made the world a better place?

31. If you punish someone and they reoffend, does that mean the punishment didn't work?

32. Is the TARDIS simply small on the outside?

33. Can you be arrogant about having saved someone's life?

34. Is being scared of nothing worse than being scared of everything?

35. Is a submarine more like a plane than a boat?

36. Would it be suicide if I chose not to get out of the way of a runaway car?

37. If it's 0°C today can it be
twice as cold tomorrow?

38. Can you measure a hole?

39. Do really clever people
use smaller words?

40. Is busking begging to music?

41. Do you control your emotions
more than they control you?

42. Is it an honourable thing
for a bee to protect its queen?

43. If you had been born taller would
you be a different person now?

44. If I disagree with you, are you a liar?

45. Can I ask your permission
to steal something from you?

46. Is the moon in the sky?

47. If the children of politicians had to serve in the armed forces, would there be fewer wars?

48. Can you be younger than your body?

49. Is flying simply delayed falling?

50. Should schools organise
school trips to abattoirs?

51. Is not going fishing a hobby?

52. Will time exist
when nothing else does?

53. Can you ever make regret go away?

54. Does coloured paper
weigh more than blank paper?

55. Is a number a description?

56. Is eating nothing but burgers
a more effective form of protest
than a hunger strike?

57. In an apartment, are your closest
neighbours the ones above you?

58. Is wind older than oil?

59. When you remember a film are you simply remembering watching the film?

60. Is every building a work of art?

61. Can you be made
to believe in God?

62. Is 'home' more of a
feeling than a place?

63. Can a pregnant woman be alone?

64. Are there any unskilled jobs?

65. Is being moral a choice?

66. Can you have saved someone's life without knowing it?

67. If you don't laugh was it not a joke?

68. Is a caterpillar a butterfly?

69. Would it be OK to have a country run by someone who wasn't from that country?

70. Can a tattoo be worth a million pounds?

71. When you look through a telescope are you looking at something close up?

72. Is a satellite photo of your country a photo with you in it?

73. Would it be better to look
in the last place you looked first?

74. Is the real you the one
your family sees on holiday?

75. Is everything an artist produces art?

76. Would you rather be fit than rich?

77. Can you pretend to be clever?

78. Is the purpose of state education to make everyone middle class?

79. Is it important to have enemies?

80. Does your life have a plot?

81. Is it stealing if the waiter leaves an item off the bill and you say nothing?

82. If you could take a pill to make you always happy, would you?

83. Can you sexually molest a robot?

84. Can you do something you didn't expect to do?

85. Is a passport photo art?

86. Is it OK to operate on a criminal's brain to stop him or her reoffending?

87. Can anything not be a toy?

88. Do you make more sense after one drink?

89. Is a pocket more of a bag than a hole?

90. Are we both watching
the same radio play?

91. Are you who you say you are?

92. Is anything not science?

93. Is conscription a form of slavery?

94. Do we all grow old at the same rate?

95. Are you responsible for the actions of your democratically elected leaders?

96. Is it more of a romantic gesture to buy someone flowers on any day but Valentine's Day?

97. Should everything be free?

98. Does water float?

99. Can you miss a train you
didn't know was leaving?

100. Do we grow tomatoes?

101. Does your dog train
you to throw sticks for it?

102. Are trees part of a community?

103. Is 0 cm a height in the same way that 0°C is a temperature?

104. If McDonald's spent billions rescuing the Sumatran tiger from extinction, should they then be allowed to sell McSumatran Tiger Burgers?

105. Can you hurry love?

106. Is the media's first priority itself?

107. Are soldiers terrorists?

108. Does a snowflake have a design?

109. Can you get lost if you don't know where you're going?

110. Can you choose to like a work of art?

111. Is a table more real than love?

112. Can a person with nothing be greedy?

113. When you remember something for the second time are you remembering the memory?

114. If you watch a film with subtitles
are you doing the acting too?

115. If I borrow a million
pounds am I a millionaire?

116. Do you use less of your memory by
using more of your phone's memory?

117. Would you rather be a
brave fool than a clever coward?

118. Does 'following orders'
let you off the hook?

119. Was anything telescopic before telescopes?

120. Is creativity
more about
making stuff up than
making stuff?

121. Can you not be part of a community?

122. Are you who your dog thinks you are?

123. Should we be made
to live longer if we can?

124. Can you wash a hole?

125. Is food made of food?

126. Can something not work
better than something else?

127. Is it more important to do
'I love you' than to say 'I love you'?

128. If the baby doesn't wake up can I
genuinely say I've been babysitting?

129. Are we taught what to be scared of?

130. Does your employer
own your thoughts?

131. Does an ant on an elephant know it better than you do from watching a TV programme about it?

132. If 'love is an energy', are all other feelings too?

133. Is 'untidy' the
natural state of a house?

134. Is bullshit better than certainty?

135. Is an entrepreneur single
(even if they're married)?

136. Am I richer because I'm smarter?

137. Do you ever really own an umbrella?

138. Do ideas come from
inside your head?

139. Do you see what I see?

140. If you don't vote, are you more
responsible for the winner of an
election than the loser?

141. Does a bishop have more
of a choice than a soldier?

142. Are you the same person at the end
of the day as you were at the beginning?

143. Do your ancestors not know what loud really is?

144. Can you change your mind?

145. Does a four-legged animal use twice as much energy going up a hill as a two-legged one?

146. Do you love a family member less after they have died?

147. Is it a joke before you get to the punchline?

148. Would it be wrong to have an avatar of yourself make love to another avatar of yourself in a virtual world?

149. Is a cat rude for not expressing gratitude?

150. When a film scares you,
is the fear imaginary?

151. Should the victim of the crime take
part in the punishment of the criminal?

152. Could you kill yourself
as an experiment?

153. Can you make
someone be your friend?

154. Is turning your back in
silence a better protest than
shouting and throwing things?

155. Can you clean dirt?

156. Can you make somewhere feel like home?

157. Could you have a war without anyone dying?

158. Is a bark a word?

159. Does everything happen for a reason in space?

160. Are you still all the people you've ever been?

161. Is getting ill a choice?

162. Do animals have an imagination?

163. Should you never take
comedians seriously?

164. Is your personality
different from your identity?

165. Is doing your duty a choice?

166. Is it impossible to
do something random?

167. Does the horizon become higher when the tide goes out?

168. Can something not happen twice?

169. Do you need to love your partner in the same way that they love you?

170. If you have two different foods in your mouth do you have three tastes?

171. Is a tree made of wood?

172. Are all interactions with children a form of grooming?

173. Is it the same song backwards?

174. Should protests be orderly?

175. Is a bat more of a
bird than a penguin is?

176. Do you own the
view from your house?

177. If you do something wrong when
you are drunk should you feel less guilty
than if you had done it stone-cold sober?

178. Should you live each
life as if it were your last?

179. Are you more likely to find God in a hospital than in a church or temple?

180. If you're happy to have a cake but sad when it's all gone, does that mean the more you eat, the sadder you get?

181. Did dragons come before dragonflies?

182. If you paint a room does
the room become smaller?

183. Is love invisible?

184. Is a mirror more of a
window than a door is?

185. If marriage is a legal
state, is adultery a crime?

186. Is there a difference between driving through the countryside and driving in the countryside?

187. Can you not like your best friend?

188. Do you decide whether it's art and not the artist?

189. Can you have the last word by remaining silent?

190. If you give a beggar a pound are you paying him or her to beg?

191. Is it wrong to have sex with an 'underage' inflatable doll?

192. Could you pretend to love someone?

193. Is vandalising a speed camera the same as vandalising a lifebuoy by a river?

194. Is music more beautiful when beautiful people play it?

195. If I read the English translation, you read the Spanish translation and someone else reads the original in Latin, are we all reading the same book?

196. Does wine taste better if you know exactly where it has come from?

197. Is a car on the back of a lorry travelling down the motorway at 60 mph parked?

198. Is handing your criminal
child over to the police a greater
act of love than not doing so?

199. Is it always OK to punch a Nazi?

200. Is it easier to be friends
with someone like you?

201. Is black a colour?

202. Is childbirth hard on the father?

203. Do I weigh less just after I spit?

204. Would your life be different if you'd had the internet in your school exams?

205. Is your hairstyle art?

206. Do you still own the things you've lost forever?

207. Should countries be run by a panel of experts?

208. Is anger a better force for good than happiness?

209. Are tall people better at telling the weather?

210. Can you be proud of
something you didn't do?

211. Is love an opinion?

212. Does a pillow hold you?

213. Is the person who designs
the bomb more innocent than
the person who drops the bomb?

214. Can you always be
sure you have a head?

215. Can you explain something you can't put into words?

216. Can a tree change how you feel?

217. Do you think when you're asleep?

218. Is a torturer more
evil than a murderer?

219. Should you lick your
dog to show your love for it?

220. Is having free will a choice?

221. Does who made it
affect whether you like it?

222. Is a lift more vehicle than room?

223. Can you touch the wind?

224. Is indifference the opposite of love rather than hate?

225. Would you have better taste if you were wealthier?

226. Can you make a wall out of glass?

227. Is it easier to be wrong than ignorant?

228. Does your house weigh more just before you vacuum it?

229. Is there less 'outdoors' in the world every time someone builds a new conservatory?

230. Can you make yourself be happy?

231. Is a sheet of red paper blank?

232. Do The Beatles exist?

233. Can you forgive someone who claims they are innocent?

234. Is it more the case that
they behave like that because they
own a BMW than they own a BMW
because they behave like that?

235. Can you look at
something you can't see?

236. Could one word be a book?

237. Is every marriage a gamble?

238. Should food be
cheaper for poor people?

239. Would you be cleverer in a different room?

240. If you didn't
mean to, is it OK?

241. Is anyone not dying?

242. Could you give up religion for Lent?

243. Does a mirror stop working
when you turn the lights off?

244. Can something be the best thing that
ever happened to you as well as the worst?

245. Does a dog mind
what you stroke it with?

246. Are you as unique
as you think you are?

247. If I have a problem with
my brain that makes me do
bad things am I a bad person?

248. Are you only as clever
as the language you use?

249. Does an air freshener
do the opposite?

250. Can you watch time?

251. Would you rather have a very old doctor than a very young one?

252. If someone makes you wait 30 minutes, have they given you 30 minutes as opposed to taken 30 minutes from you?

253. Can everyone wear exclusive clothes?

254. If they made the 9 o'clock news twice as long, would there be twice as much news?

255. Should paedophiles be allowed to speak to virtual reality 'children'?

256. In a horse race are the horses racing?

257. Is it OK for a self-driving car to kill its occupants to save at least one more person than the number of people in the car?

258. Is it easier to dance for ten minutes than run for ten minutes?

259. Can a baby be stupid?

260. Is a beautiful photo simply an ordinary photo of a beautiful thing?

261. Is putting a convicted criminal in prison a form of revenge?

262. If history has taught us anything, is it that we never learn anything from history?

263. Can a non-racist person tell a racist joke?

264. Can being sad make you happy?

265. Are you a different person when you're speaking a different language?

266. Do any of your opinions originate from within your own mind?

267. If you dream of someone who has died, are you dreaming of their ghost?

268. Can you deliberately set off a policeman's hunch?

269. Is the North Pole where south starts?

270. Are you a good person if you
save more lives than you take?

271. Do people who don't believe
in God know He doesn't exist?

272. Do you attract
rather than make money?

273. With more humans in the world than
ever before, are there fewer molecules
available to be made into other things?

274. Can you love someone you don't like?

275. Can you have
an invisible toy?

276. Is believing
God exists a stronger
sentiment than
knowing He doesn't?

277. Is everything made of something?

278. Can you lose successfully?

279. Do you need somebody to love?

280. Can a river die?

281. Is our character more the
result of what we haven't done
than what we have done?

282. Were you loved less when
your younger sibling was born?

283. Is it better to look lustfully at
someone's beautiful spouse than not to?

284. Could a pet think you were its pet?

285. Should the jury always be
the same colour as the accused?

286. Are you ever thinking
what I'm thinking?

287. Is your house part of your family?

288. Is the telescope a more important invention than the microscope?

289. Can you add one
to an infinite number?

290. Are you a different person
once both your parents have died?

291. Is a colour a thing?

292. Can you dance to silence?

293. Can a robot be kind?

294. Does school encourage
you to be selfish?

295. Is facial hair a form
of make-up for men?

296. Does one theft make you a thief?

297. If the cure for cancer meant
constructing a huge factory in
Antarctica, should we do it anyway?

298. Is going there
and back two journeys?

299. Is a pen to a word what a drill is to a hole?

300. Can you be
accidentally evil?

301. Is a strong opposition more important to democracy than the government?

302. Would you rather have no money than no emotions?

303. If you are locked out of your car, is it broken down?

304. Are there more colours than things?

305. Is it vain to keep looking in the mirror because you like how ugly you appear?

306. Is the Earth biodegradable?

307. If I sit on a train facing forwards
will I have a different journey than
if I sit facing the other way?

308. Should stupid people
be allowed to vote?

309. Can you prove that
all zebras have stripes?

310. Is it easier to criticise
something than to praise it?

311. Is a West End musical more like real life than a Shakespearean tragedy?

312. Would you
be twice as happy
if you won the
Lottery twice?

313. Does something become
a memory as it happens?

314. Do clocks think?

315. Is 'climb a tree' a suitable task
to be given to a child as homework?

316. Can you say for sure that
there will be a scrum in the
rugby match that's just started?

317. Does it matter who you love?

318. Is a shadow a hole?

319. Does changing your underwear change your personality?

320. Do animals have hobbies?

321. Does swearing in a foreign language count as swearing?

322. Is it the same road in both directions?

323. If the teacher knows what's going to happen, is it still an experiment?

324. Is a snail's shell more of a prison than a home?

325. Do you die when the last person who remembers you dies?

326. Can you hoover with a Dyson?

327. When you train a dog, are the words you use more for your benefit than the dog's?

328. Is a lump of rock a rock?

329. Do people marry people who are as ugly as they are?

330. Does it matter who or what is
on the other end when you're sexting?

331. If we're not all
doomed, should we be?

332. Can I buy a pound
from you for a pound?

333. Can a crime be beautiful?

334. If workers live, work and sleep
in the iPhone factory, could you
claim that iPhones are 'home-made'?

335. Are clothes less dirty after they have been on the bedroom floor for a week than when you took them off?

336. Is equality the same as fairness?

337. Is it an act of love to
let your partner die first?

338. Can you experience
fear without being scared?

339. If it's rude to stare at people
who look different from us, would
it be better to turn our backs?

340. Is any wealth created
without exploitation?

341. Is it the same room
with the lights off?

342. Would you accept a
heart transplant from a rapist?

343. Are you controlled by forces
you don't know anything about?

344. Is a car more like a piece
of clothing than a bicycle is?

345. Does anyone deserve to die?

346. When you switch a light off,
does the part of the room nearest
the bulb go dark first?

347. Is it undemocratic to be made to vote?

348. Can you tell the difference between a dream and the memory of a dream?

349. Is your mind the oldest part of you?

350. Would you play the Lottery if there was more chance of winning but also of losing everything?

351. Is your father who you think he is?

352. Is it more important to be right than to be nice?

353. Is a garden man-made?

354. Is not hitting a rabbit with
your car the same as saving its life?

355. Are the bubbles in the
bottle before you open it?

356. Does it matter what they think?

357. Do you miss a loved one more
the farther they are away from you?

358. If I lose £2, then find £1, am I lucky?

359. Can you be
rude to yourself?

360. Is a bad government better for citizenship than a good government?

361. Can you have an
argument with an echo?

362. Is my God your God?

363. If you built a railway line that did
converge on the horizon, could you tell?

364. If you stopped dusting would the
dust eventually stop accumulating?

365. Is it your duty to love your children?

366. Is a freedom fighter a terrorist
if someone else says they are?

367. Would it be wrong to have sex with
a sheep in an online virtual world?

368. If you don't empty the
dishwasher, is it a cupboard?

369. Is your diary of future plans
more important than your
diary of things you've done?

370. Are you only ever
truly yourself naked?

371. Can a work of art have no meaning?

372. Should we just love criminals more rather than punish them?

373. Can you be afraid of fairies?

374. Can the best thing about a radio station be the music it doesn't play?

375. Is it better to die suddenly than be given a month to live?

376. If you watch a play where the second half is the same as the first half, have you seen two plays not one?

377. Can a fruit annoy you?

378. Do you use your imagination when you dream?

379. Can you win an argument with yourself?

380. Can any member of the Rolling Stones be part of a Rolling Stones tribute band?

381. Would a turd look nicer in an ornate gold frame?

382. Does your dog know what it did last summer?

383. Is it harder to bear when you are in a position to do something than it is when you are in a position to do nothing?

384. Do you have
the same number of
thoughts each day?

385. Do animals have friends?

386. If you put on weight
does it change who you are?

387. Should exams test what you
can do rather than what you can't?

388. Would it be better to blow your nose
into a plastic bag rather than a hanky?

389. Should people in positions
of authority be fit and healthy?

390. Is it always better out than in?

391. Is taking pity on
someone a good thing?

392. Should walking across hot coals
be part of the school curriculum?

393. Can you ever go
to the same place twice?

394. Can you love someone you can't see?

395. Does who you meet change who you are?

396. Is the public
ultimately helpless?

397. Is anything not art?

398. If you can be brainwashed,
can you also be soulwashed?

399. Would a poet in space tell you more
about space than a scientist in space?

400. Can a baby experience beauty?

401. In a multicultural society should
different laws apply to different people?

402. Does a guide dog
know where it's going?

403. Is a baby poor?

404. If you were identified as
being genetically inclined to do
bad things should you be locked
up before you do them?

405. Would you be someone
else if you had grown up
speaking a different language?

406. Is it the same family when
you have a new family member?

407. Can you fit a crowd into a phone box?

408. Does the Church need the poor?

409. Do you have to respect the President?

410. Is sadness more contagious than happiness?

411. Can we agree on how to pronounce '&'?

412. Is ego another word for confidence?

413. If you see someone being bullied should you feel guilty if you do nothing about it?

414. Can you choose to be bored?

415. Does love come from
outside you rather than inside?

416. Is it bad luck if your cat
does a crap in the shower tray?

417. Do we all see the same mountain?

418. Is a 'yes/no' or 'in/out' referendum
the worst way of deciding anything?

419. Is art more about getting rid of what's there than creating something?

420. Can you
be nowhere?

421. If you did something drunk that you would never have done sober, can you blame the alcohol?

422. Are children born happy?

423. Is caving an outdoor sport?

424. Is cynicism the opposite of optimism more than pessimism is?

425. Can you see something you can't describe in words?

426. Is leadership all about getting people to do things you want them to do but they don't?

427. Should parents be fined for having unfit children?

428. Is a murderer evil if they are just doing their job?

429. Is a blocked drain a drain?

430. Do you choose your emotions?

431. Can you know
if your dog thinks
about you when
you're at work?

432. Is school the place to go to learn to know your place?

433. If religion were banned would there be more good in the world?

434. Do you use your senses to experience that Christmassy feeling?

435. Is a prison a hotel you can't leave?

436. Do guns kill people?

437. Is it a lie if you believe it?

438. Do we decide what is the new normal as opposed to accepting it?

439. Is civil disobedience something a democratic government should encourage?

440. Are some horses worth more than some humans?

441. Is the silence between the notes music?

442. Do all your family members have to be alive to be part of your family?

443. Can you enjoy beauty without love?

444. Can you be sure that someone is wrong, even though you don't know why?

445. If we're all the same, do we know who we're the same as?

446. Are my facts truer than yours?

447. Are children responsible for what they eat and drink?

448. Should you respect the person in charge simply because they're in charge?

449. If a bully threatens you should you cry and scream like a baby so they don't bother, rather than being big and strong and letting them hit you?

450. Should the jury have their backs
to the accused, like in *The Voice*?

451. Can you be proud
to have lost your ego?

452. Does wind have a size?

453. If you shine a candle in a mirror
do you get twice as much light?

454. Is love scientific?

455. Are you smarter with your smartphone?

456. Do you need to be brave to operate a military drone?

457. Should vegans not listen to musicians who use strings made from animal gut on their instruments?

458. Are you a different person with your clothes off?

459. Would it change anything if God were a woman?

460. Are we made of food?

461. Would you rather win a hundred friends than a hundred pounds?

462. Are there any
emotions dogs don't have?

463. If we all kept the safe
distance from the car in front
would motorways have to be longer?

464. Is history best left in the past?

465. Can you dance badly to silence?

466. Are you in love with your family?

467. If it didn't harm you was it dangerous?

468. Is east the opposite of west, in the same way that north is the opposite of south?

469. Should civil unrest
be taught at school?

470. Is your soul the same age you are?

471. Would you be a different
person now if one of your
parents had had a different job?

472. If a robot waiter brings you
a drink should you say thank you?

473. Are ancestors you've
never met part of your family?

474. Can you store clean clothes
all over your bedroom floor?

475. Is 'Love is God' a better
notion than 'God is Love'?

476. Can a fly see a skyscraper?

477. Do you know what
a mermaid looks like?

478. Does the difference between a flood
and a puddle depend on how big you are?

479. Does the depletion of fish stocks help mitigate against the rise in sea levels?

480. Can anything
be a house?

481. If I 'hold your coat',
am I to blame too?

482. Can a bed communicate?

483. Can you be scared of something
that is actually happening?

484. Should you be the partner
your partner deserves?

485. Is it easier to make a
name for yourself these days by
standing on the throats of giants?

486. If you turn your speaker upside down, does the sound come out upside down?

487. Do you need a high boredom threshold to be clever?

488. Can you always be sure you're not doing any harm?

489. Do photographs distort your memories?

490. For children to know right from wrong do they have to be told what's right and what's wrong?

491. If I stick a bunch of flowers in a computer does the computer become a vase?

492. Are stars there?

493. Is a global water shortage caused by too many people, not by a shortage of water?

494. Is it OK to bully a bully?

495. Is a spider more of an architect than a builder?

496. Is it worth watching the match if you don't care who wins?

497. Is 'tunnel' another word for 'bridge'?

498. Would you give blood if there were a possibility that it would save the life of a paedophile?

499. Is a tree free?

500. If humans are the only racist species, is it for a reason?

501. Do all animals have a version of 'childhood'?

502. Should euthanasia be granted to those who are so ill, they no longer have the ability to take their own life?

503. Did humans
invent time?

504. Is a dog
always honest?

505. Can you hear silence?

506. If you drop a sweet wrapper
in your front room, is it litter?

507. Is a computer more like
a cupboard than a brain?

508. Can you have too many friends?

509. Do you need to be a parent
to be a good education minister?

510. Does a jellyfish know where it's going?

511. Should you always tell the truth
at a funeral but never at a wedding?

512. Does the history taught in
its schools determine the sort
of society a country ends up with?

513. Is it worse to slap a
child than to torture a cat?

514. If your handwriting is an
extension of your personality, is it
the same when you use emoticons?

515. Do ants have more freedom than children?

516. Can you be racist against your own race?

517. Is it the same journey if you change the soundtrack?

518. Can you set out to fail?

519. Is a tree helpless?

520. Is smoking a form of euthanasia?

521. Is being alive a choice?

522. Should you always bring
your boss solutions, not problems?

523. Is a frozen pizza food?

524. Can you miss the
enemy you used to have?

525. Does the sky weigh
more on a cloudy day?

526. Should we grade prospective
politicians rather than vote for them?

527. Are you smarter than your smartphone?

528. When you look for an answer, do you create it rather than find it?

529. Is your soul the same size as when you were a baby?

530. For every original song written is there one original song fewer that can be written?

531. Is giving a burger to a vegetarian beggar a charitable act?

532. Does a unicorn have more horns than a pixie?

533. If I tell you I am lying, am I a liar?

534. Is architecture
'building with people'?

535. If you've never been drunk
have you never been the real you?

536. If you read a newspaper in a shop
without paying for it, is that stealing?

537. Is the moment when you can't
see the car's indicator as important
as the moment when you can?

538. Can a poem written
by a robot be great art?

539. Do we use question marks in speech?

540. Have you stopped becoming you yet?

541. Is eating food when you're full less wasteful than throwing it away?

542. Is overtaking the same as jumping the queue?

543. Should school for poor people be about trying to help them be wealthier?

544. Is it really better to have loved and lost than never to have loved at all?

545. If you feed a terrorist, are you a terrorist too?

546. Is it easier to spot someone else's ignorance than your own?

547. Do birds make music?

548. Would you be a different person if you'd chosen a different career?

549. Can a dog insult you?

550. If you've heard it before is it no longer funny?

551. Can you put rubbish in a litter bin?

552. Is being strong the same as refusing to be weak?

553. Do you achieve more
if you don't care?

554. Can a dead person be rich?

555. Are lions more
important than worms?

556. Do you need a good
imagination to be scared?

557. Can you visit your own home?

558. Does the cup of tea taste
the same in a different mug?

559. Is justifying terrorism
the same as condoning it?

560. Is 'unemotional' another
way of saying 'lacks imagination'?

561. Would a baby born on
a deserted island ever laugh?

562. Can you steal someone's rubbish?

563. Is leaving a cold cup of tea in the living room twice as bad as leaving half a cup of cold tea there?

564. Is not being against racism the same as being for it?

565. If there were no weapons
would there be no wars?

566. Are your neighbours
still your neighbours when
they're on their holidays?

567. Do we see more by going
nowhere than by travelling far afield?

568. Can you be busy waiting?

569. Should we be allowed to harpoon
any animal for research purposes?

570. If you are not like
me are you not normal?

571. Was a broken promise a lie?

572. Can you be an expert on unicorns?

573. Can you love someone a bit?

574. Is there anything you
couldn't have a museum about?

575. Is a tidy room bigger than a messy room?

576. Does life
get its ideas
from the movies?

577. Can you be truly happy
if you are aspirational?

578. Can we solve
problems we can't state?

579. Is a crime committed against
you worse if it is committed by
someone not like you?

580. You may know what you like, but do
you know why you like what you like?

581. Would childhood be better if
children didn't have to go to school?

582. If the water in the river
changes all the time can you say
exactly what or where the river is?

583. Can it be your destiny
to do the wrong thing?

584. Should you be paid compensation
by the obese person next to you for the
amount of your airline seat they take up?

585. If I discovered a cure for cancer,
but didn't want to share my discovery
with the world, should I be made to?

586. Can you design something with two
wheels, pedals and a seat that isn't a bicycle?

587. When you think in your dream, are you thinking?

588. Is perfume a form of deception?

589. Can anything with a
brain get a headache?

590. Should everyone be made to be a
nurse for a year when they're 18?

591. Can you be as sure that
something you can't see doesn't
exist as you can be that it does?

592. Can you be part of a
community without knowing it?

593. Does keeping up with what's
happening in the news change anything?

594. Are babies born with their emotions?

595. If you found a contraceptive
in your teenage child's room,
should you be pleased?

596. Is the first aeroplane ever
built a greater technological
innovation than the last one built?

597. Do you own money?

598. If you can't do anything about
it should you do nothing about it?

599. Can you 'fight for' without 'fighting against'?

600. Can you
see a mountain
from the top?

601. When you measure the area of a rectangle, are you measuring the rectangular space that isn't rectangle?

602. Is happiness something you take?

603. Do you own your children?

604. Is there such a thing as a senseless act?

605. Should we take it in turns to run the country?

606. Are socks essentially
solitary creatures?

607. Can food make you sad?

608. If feeding a terrorist makes
you a terrorist, does making them
a cup of tea have the same effect?

609. Can something stop not happening?

610. Is a fairy story truer
than a newspaper story?

611. Can you ever be too happy?

612. Is an inflated balloon lighter than a deflated balloon?

613. Should all the money in the world be redistributed equally at the beginning of every new year?

614. Does a child have more freedom than an adult?

615. Do masochistic sinners go to heaven?

616. Can you ever be lonely if you've never been in love?

617. Is anything worth dying for?

618. If a Rolls-Royce were dangling above a canyon by a thread, would the thread be more valuable than the Rolls-Royce?

619. Is torture natural?

620. Does your nationality have more influence over your behaviour than you do?

621. Is the park bench yours to share?

622. Can you celebrate not eating cake by not eating cake?

623. Are you your history?

624. Would you know if you didn't have a mind?

625. If I know more than you,
am I cleverer than you?

626. If they didn't show up,
were you waiting for them?

627. Should we let people into
the queue directly behind us?

628. Is this it ...?